THE MINDSET

You are what you think

Raymond Delmut Na'anlep

Prepared for print by

Preflight Books, Pretoria,

www.preflightbooks.co.za

Layout by

Aimèe Armstrong

Cover design by

Alexander Moolman

ISBN - 13

978-0-620-75973-1

CONTENTS

Message

I am a book with a message that quickens the mind of every person who reads me with a great penchant. Allow me to interact with you because I am not just a mere piece of literary work. Rather accept the messages encrypted on every page as mind-transforming resources presented in the form of short, but well-explained, meaningful and wise quotes.

Read me meditatively with a positive perception to get a whole chunk of life-impacting information. The ultimate goal of the message is for you to maximize every potential and undertake great exploits in all endeavours through reactivating your thought patterns.

Likewise, be a goal-getter. Read one quote at a time and substantiate it before moving to the next one. So, become inspired as you read through me because only the mind defines our life.

THE MINDSET

Preface

The mind is perhaps the most crucial part of the make-up of any human. The reason is that the mind defines each person. For example, a toddler that is handicapped in some way that is not physical will be noticed by the adults around it. Even long before the child can talk, if they have a defect, for example autism, it will be noticed in their actions which is an output of their mind. Equally, the state of the mind of an adult will also be known in the way they make decisions and take action. The mind is where thought processes take place, and the consequences of the thought processes are the actions taken. Those actions, in turn have consequences; they determine what happens around you, and the direction your life takes – positive or negative.

Personally, I changed my mind after watching the UEFA Soccer League final match played between two German teams – Borussia Dortmund and Bayern Munich at the Wembley Stadium, London, in 2013. You see, the Bayern Munich coach had been trying for years to get that trophy. Though he got close on a few occasions and failed, he still didn't give up on his set goal of winning the trophy; after which, he planned to retire. When he eventually won, I developed a new mindset, which inspired the writing of this book.

Also, I had a lingering health challenge for some time, but then I realized that the mindset I had towards it would either take me out of it, or keep me there.

So, I decided to change my thoughts and approach to life, not only for my health's sake, but for my work and life's sake in general. I also decided to share the power and light I had seen in having a positive mindset towards every situation I face. I realized that you are a direct product of your thoughts. Temptation, distraction and failure are all forms and products of your mind or thoughts.

So, this book is not written for the sake of writing; it is meant to share with the reader all my experiences and how it worked out for me. In the book, the power that the mind has in channelling the course of life for any human is focussed on. The book intends to make you realize that if you are in charge of your mind, you are in charge of your life. In addition, the benefit of a mind that's positively channelled is given attention. I hope you find it beneficial.

Raymond Delmut, January 2016

Dedication

This book is dedicated to my parents, Mr and Mrs Raymond Delmut, who, though not educated, gave me the best formal education that brought me this far. Most of all, I dedicate this book to the almighty God who gives the inspiration and knowledge that is in a book; to Him be the glory.

Foreword

"Men at the top are men of words. Your measure in life is determined by the measure of the words you have in you."

Delmut awakens the slumbering, strengthens the weak, encourages the downcast and kindles within a mighty desire for all round fulfilment.

The inspirational values were drawn from the infinite intelligence which is the furniture of our mind; Ray was illuminated with the reality that these jewels will shape our thinking from our conscience and direct our actions.

Raymond Delmut Na'anlep set a value upon his words by offering invincible provisions that will redefine the quality of our mindsets in all aspects of life. In his words, "thought is the oldest philosophy of life because every created thing emerged from a thought."

The Mindset is a must read for all those who need to create a better world for themselves. "The value you attach to your words will determine how others will sense their value."

Professor Solomon Omayiwa

Acknowledgements

Thanks and immense appreciation to my parents; my elder brother, Vincent Daniang Raymond, for the support and sponsorship; and my other siblings for their encouragement and prayers.

To my wife, Martina Raymond Na'anlep, for moral support and standing by me; to my friend, Don Ady, for encouragement and connections that make this book possible; to my friend, Walshak Samuel, for compiling this book and, for painstakingly making this book a reality. To all other well-wishers in my life, I say a big thank you.

Author's Note

The mind is the only resource that is relevant in every economy and in every sector of the economy.

My ultimate goal in this book is to achieve a certain level of originality as a young African writer.

My writing is not for mere fame, cheap popularity, fortune or intellectualism, but for the purpose of making a global impact among members of the entire human race.

Raymond Delmut

What is a mindset?

What is the mind? The mind is seen as the part of you that makes you able to be aware of things, to think and to feel. The mind is also considered as a part of you that gives you the ability to think and reason, or even as a person's intelligence.

What the mind is can also be understood from other perspectives and disciplines. But what is important for us to note here is that more than any other factor, the mind plays such a powerful part in the course of any person's life.

A mindset is a belief that you have either about yourself, or other issues that concern you. It is a fixed mental attitude or disposition which often predetermines your response to a situation and how you interpret the situation. Mindset can also be seen as your inclinations, tendencies, or habits.

It's important to realize that a mindset influences you even more than the formal education you have received; it goes beyond the talent you have. In fact, a mindset can make the most educated person behave in an unexpected manner that's well below their standards.

They can reason in a way that will confound others. Many have a good education, but their mindset is a source of setback for them. The point is that the mind can make or destroy you. But it is also the greatest asset to use to your advantage or ignore at your own risk. It's because actions that result from a change of mindset will, in turn, lead to a change in the course of your life.

Meanwhile, note that the words 'mind' and 'mindset' are used interchangeably in the course of our discourse. The effect your mindset has on your life is amazing if only you realize it. It's because every word you utter, and the steps you take are conceived first in the mind.

Your mind is, therefore, like a walking stick that a physically impaired person uses to lead him; where the stick indicates solid ground is the direction his feet follow.

Definition

Mindset is a belief about yourself and your most basic quality. Mindset is a fixed mental attitude or disposition that predetermines your responses to an interpretation of a situation, inclination, or a habit.

The Mindset is a book intended to help everyone cultivate and develop a positive and growing mindset that can enhance new ideas, innovations and inventions in the diverse spheres of human activities, ranging from the works of art and entertainment, science and technology, to sports and business. The idea of this book is geared towards enriching, renovating, rebranding, remodelling, reforming and transforming the minds of both old and young to be able to see and convert every immaterial resource to material wealth as found in every nation, or country of the world.

The Mindset goes beyond mere education and talent to tell us how the mind is key in stimulating growth, and the achievement of goals and objectives. The Mindset calls our attention to the fact that success can be attained through reactivating the appropriate thought pattern.

In this book, you will see where it is prescribed as a therapy for depression, stagnation, discouragement, and failure. The book is recommended for teaching simple psychology of the mind. The main emphasis is that the mind of man is a great asset for different uses. After reading The Mindset which is meant to bring about social, financial, political, and psychological transformation, the book will also give everyone a new direction in life in general.

Please note, the decisions which result in a change of mind will, in turn, lead to a change of purpose and action.

This book is meant to teach the simple psychology of success and greatness through positive mindset or thought. The Mindset is a book that intends to highlight the relevance of intrapersonal communication and how it applies to life in its entirety.

How the mindset is formed

Parents – Various factors inform your mindset, but the earliest are your parents. Parental upbringing is important in the life of anyone. It's from a parent that a child receives information that shapes their earlier pattern of thinking.

Friends – Friends or peer groups are other forms of channels by which information is fed into the mind. Some positions and beliefs are simply from the power of the word uttered by people you are close to. They raise arguments either based on their experience, or what they have also heard. If this is negative, it can set up wrong notions in the mind of their listener(s).

Education – Education is a major channel by which the mind is fed with information. The effect of this is obvious all around. For example, there is a system of education in which every student is made to feel that after leaving school, searching for a job in an office is the way to go. That has produced millions of youths who don't develop the talent in them that can make them an employer.

Cultural orientation – The culture in which you find yourself is crucial to how your mindset is formed. As it is, many culturally-formed beliefs are based on myth, established biases, wrong notions, or tradition that sometimes has no proven basis.

The strength of culture is often drawn from the claim that, "this is how the forefathers did it," and what the forefathers did must always be the pattern, even when it obviously can't be sustained in contemporary changed times. What one feeds on: what you personally feed yourself; is also crucial.

This is not about food; it's about the information - negative or positive - the idea,the belief, and known ways of doing things that inform your mind. Many watch films and all they see is a life of comfort which they believe is the reality. The films show a life of luxury, fast cars, and exotic mansions, but not often the hard work, the integrity, the honesty, the dedication, or the sweat that goes into making the acquisition of luxury possible. Many don't improve their minds by reading books for self-development because what they do read also misinforms their minds. Many who can look inside them and bring out their ability in one field or the other, don't bother to do so because of the negativity that society has made them believe.

What they feed on combine to make their view on most matters what it is. You cannot be better than what you feed yourself.

Functions of the mindset

Your mindset can do the following:

It can propel. The thought process that precedes action is not doubted.

The mind is where an idea is conceived and processed, and action follows. When the thought process is positive, the steps that follow are positive. When it is negative, the actions that follow are negative.

The propelling power of the mind can't be ignored when it comes to the direction in which your life moves, and that is why your mindset needs to be the best it can be. It determines the course your life takes – the summation of one's actions determines the shape one's life takes.

The person who thinks something is possible will consistently embark on endeavours and eventually come through. On the other hand, the individual who views challenges as impossible missions will not get anything done. In the process, what should be confronted to lift him is left untouched, that way he remains a failure or an underachiever.

- It determines your view – The mind processes what the mouth says. The position you take on any issue is evident of the thought process. The view you have about an issue tends to become a label by which you are defined or described.

- Thus, you could be said to be 'conservative' if your view is that things should evolve slowly, or that the status quo should be maintained. You may also be labelled as 'moderate', depending on your position as to whether a course of action should either be too far to the right, or too far to the left. You may also be called 'radical' if you want change to happen no matter what it costs.

- It can deny - Mindset can deny you many things. This is because mindset informs attitude and belief. Belief that is not right may make you miss out on what you should get.

- An example of this, is the belief that people from a particular ethnic group are bad can lead to your missing out on your helper, or the person who can introduce you to where you can get what you are looking for.

- Yet whatever you are looking for is in the hands of another human being. The key to whichever door you want to open is already in the hands of one person or another irrespective of tribe or religion. Meanwhile, a mindset that is unnecessarily biased may make you miss it. A mindset that is wrong can deny you the needed assistance in life.

- It can lift – Mindset that is right can lead to lifting. If you have a positive mind, you'll see possibilities even where there are impossibilities. You'll see a challenge that can be overcome where others see a problem. You'll see a mountain that can lift you up above others, while others see it as a barrier. The fact is; your mountain is your stepping stone to greater heights. Mountains lift and take higher. But your mindset is the determinant of whether this happens or not.

WHEN THE MINDSET IS POSITIVE

A positive mindset refuses to accept difficulty in totality

Many people imagine difficulties and these imaginations become a reality in real-life issues. Nothing is difficult except what you picture or conceive as difficult in the realm of the mind or in your thoughts. The real-life difficulty is just a direct application of what is already preconceived in the mind.

There is nothing difficult except a negative mindset, which perpetually conceives everything as impossible and difficult. A positive mindset is the key to solving all life problems and can equally convert them in to opportunities. A positive mindset can see opportunities where others cannot. A positive mindset can see beyond difficulties and has the power to force such obstacles to give way for opportunities to prevail. A positive mindset refuses to accept difficulty in totality. Positive thoughts have the ability to open each and every difficult door.

A positive twist in your thoughts will open new doors of opportunity for you. Those who know how to control their mind, or their thought faculties, have the ability to unlock the doors of success. Every step of success is tied to the way in which the mind is utilized to deliberate a good plan. Good plans are a product of the mind.

The mind is the powerhouse of a person in which every great and good thing and remarkable success lies. Therefore, those who know the secret are on top of the world as celebrities today, while others are just spectators; wondering how the successful are making magic. It means that greatness lies in the mind. The mind is the key to unlocking difficult doors.

 IF YOU UNDERSTAND YOUR MIND,
YOU WILL INVARIABLY UNDERSTAND LIFE

The mastery of the mind is automatically a mastery of life

Life is programmed and embedded deep in our thoughts or minds. A clear picture of the mindset will always give a clear picture of what to do in life in its entirety. The simple reason is because the mind dictates what happens to us in life. So, without good understanding or full control of what goes on in your mind, life will become an accident.

A mastery of the mind is automatically a mastery of life. You are down simply because you have negative thought faculties and a low self-esteem. The ability to guide your thoughts means that you have the ability to guide your life. It is what you think that makes you behave the way you do. Bad actions come from bad decisions, and bad thoughts produce a bad person. The mind determines your relevance in life.

The inability to control the mind will result in the inability to have control over the affairs of life. A proper understanding of what goes on in the mind will help in understanding life in general.

A quality life only comes from quality thoughts. Life lies right inside the mind because the mind gives meaning to life in general; it means that any understanding of the mind will ultimately result in understanding how to go about life in general..

The inability to understand what goes on in the mind will result in a lack of understanding of how to manage life's affairs. The wisdom that can interpret the mind can likewise interpret all of life's issues. If you understand the secret of the mind, you will also understand life.

STRENGTH IS NOT THE FUNCTION OF THE PHYSICAL, THE GREATEST STRENGTH OF A MAN LIES IN HIS THOUGHTS

A strong mindset alone can strengthen the survival of a person

The simple reason is that thoughts direct our decisions; it, therefore, means that only the strong in mind can withstand every challenge and intimidation that threatens the livelihood (survival) of a person. Courage is the function of the mind and not a physical attribute. A strong mindset alone can strengthen the survival of a person.

You have no strength except if you have a strong mind. There's no strong person, except a person with a strong mindset.

Every feeble-minded individual is also physically fragile. Therefore, equip your mind with bold and strong thought patterns.

Only the person who thinks they are strong is seen to manifest strength physically. Your mental picture is your mental capability, and mental capability is your physical strength. Mental strength is greater than physical strength, so the strength of your thoughts determines your strength in life.

EMPOWERED THOUGHT IS BETTER THAN THE NEED FOR FINANCIAL EMPOWERMENT

An empowered thought can generate money

An empowered mindset does not beg for financial assistance, but can rather create wealth. Empowered thoughts have the ability to translate into financial empowerment; pro-active minds belong to productive individuals who manifest very effective wealth creation.

An empowered thought results in more than financial empowerment if approached with the right mindset.

The millions given to unproductive minds is a waste of resources, while empowered minds, or thoughts, are the key to financial transformation.

Great thinkers are great assets for wealth creation. Empower your thoughts to empower your life. You don't need money to be empowered; you just need to empower your thoughts. An empowered thought can generate money. The richest man in the world is the product of a positive thought.

GREAT PEOPLE ARE GREAT THINKERS, GREAT MINDS ARE GREAT PEOPLE

Great ideas and innovations are all from great minds/thinkers

Productive minds are great achievers. Only the minds who think positively make an impact in their world. Great thinkers have track records of the major inventions in the world today. Those who think positively are successful in their generations and are always responsible for transforming the entire society.

Look at history and it is glaring that only great thinkers make an impact in this world. Great ideas and innovations are all from great minds or thinkers.

Only great thinkers make it great by doing extraordinary things as a result of a positive mindset.

People who think positively do very well in life. Examples are Bill Gates, the father of the USA's Microsoft Corporation; and Thomas Edison, who invented the light bulb. Even after failing several times, Edison refused to give up. Great thoughts produce great people.

Optimism is better than silver and gold

Positive and optimistic thinkers convert the impossible to possible with the kind of mentality they have. What is possible in the mind is equally possible in real life. The mind believes, and the belief is what becomes possible. What becomes possible is the end result or reality. Positive thoughts create the image of a thing or an event, while optimism makes it workable.

What you don't believe will never come to you, and it will always be impossible. What you think is what you become. Positive thinking produces creativity through the power of imagination; and imagination fuels optimism, while optimism is the cure for mediocrity.

Optimistic and positive thinkers imagine and believe what others don't. Optimistic people are driven by strange powers that make unusual things happen in the world. Examples are Nelson Mandela of South Africa in his tireless fight against apartheid; and Abraham Lincoln's persistence in his political career after losing several elections. But, he who later became one of the greatest presidents of the United States of America.

Optimism is better than silver and gold. It is a fertile ground for success and riches. Positive thinking conquers every obstacle and raises you above every barrier in life.

Without positive and great thinkers, there will be no innovations

No innovation or invention ever existed without a positive thought first. Every innovation and invention is first created in the realm of the mind before the physical product becomes a reality.

Think of any innovation or invention you see in the world. All are the byproducts of positive thoughts only. The aircraft you see today is exactly the mindset of the inventor. Without positive and great thinkers, there will be no innovations and inventions.

Positive thoughts create new ideas, and new ideas become innovations and inventions in the world. What you see in the mind is capable of becoming a real product in the market. Think and create a new world full of brand new products.

*The power of thought boosts self-motivation and
infinitely keeps you motivated*

Positive thoughts will naturally take you out of depression. Real motivation comes from within you and not from external sources. All forms of extrinsic motivation fade away. Intrinsic motivation emanates from inside and spurs an individual to great decisions and actions.

The only natural and permanent motivation is self-motivation through the power of positive thought. Every other source of motivation can fail, while positive thoughts remain constant. The power of thought boosts self-motivation and infinitely keeps you motivated.

If you are seriously troubled, the greatest counsel is to consult your thought faculties. Thoughts have life. What you think is what you become. Thoughts that uplift your spirit will permanently keep you motivated. Idleness is not a lack of activity, but an idle mind.

9 | WHAT YOU ARE TODAY IS AS A RESULT
OF YOUR THOUGHTS YESTERDAY

It is impossible to grow beyond your thoughts

What you will be tomorrow is determined by your thoughts today. It is impossible to grow beyond your thoughts because that is the measure of what you know and can do at the moment. The level of every success in everyone must be commensurate to the level of their thoughts, or level of awareness in life.

Where you are and what you become is all determined by the level of your thoughts yesterday, today and tomorrow, respectively. The level of your thoughts determines the level of your achievement at a particular moment in time. The past, present and future concerns of success and greatness are determined by the mindset.

Decorate and support your vision with positive thoughts

Nothing can support and sustain a vision like mindset.

Dreams and visions are abandoned or aborted due to mindset, or the extent to which the vision carrier thinks of it. What you think determines your focus, and focus determines the success and the full actualization of your vision.

A vision not strongly supported by a good mindset cannot survive or succeed. So many visions without good thought to make them succeed will die out.

Enhance and support your vision with positive thoughts to enable its survival and success. Negative thoughts are a distraction and, at the same time, destroy a vision. All visions are anchored by positive thinking.

The mind of a person is essential to their survival as a successful being. Vision is a product of thought; therefore, it needs positive thought or mindset to succeed.

 REFRAME YOUR THOUGHTS BECAUSE YOUR BODY WILL ALWAYS GO IN THE SAME DIRECTION

The thought faculties of a person are the centre of their life

If you reframe your mindset it will also reframe your life. The direction you go in life is connected to the direction of your thoughts. The mind is the remote control of the body. The body goes where the mind directs it.

What the mind tells you determines the direction you go in life. The idea to go from one place to another, one city to another, or one destination to another is decided within the realm of the mind before your body takes action. To leave the house to go to work, or pay a visit to someone is all from the mind. The physical body only complies with the direction the mind has taken.

Every reform in the mind will translate to a reform in life. If your mind is properly guided, your life will also be guided. However, any misleading in the mind can equally be a misleading in life. The mathematical terms of mindset is that the mind is equal to everything that reflects in your life, while any negativity in the mind equals failure in life. So, redirect your thoughts well. What you think in a moment determines what you do in that measurable time.

If you lack direction in your thoughts, you will definitely lack direction in life. Purging the mind means purging your life from the debris of failure. The thought faculties of persons are the centre of their life.

Think right and you will do things right; think wrong and you will then do things wrong. Reframe your thoughts because you will always go in the same direction as that of your mindset.

Positive thoughts produce good things that
result in a positive life

Our thoughts are what control our lives, and coordinate the affairs of our lives to make them better, successful and worth living. Then, only positive thinking will result in positive living because positive begets good, while negative begets bad.

It is the mind that makes you idle, redundant, and unproductive. It is also the mind that can make you active, wise, productive, and very successful. Adopt a positive thinking pattern. Positive thoughts improve the quality of life through success and greatness. Positive thoughts produce good things that result in a positive life.

What positive thought does is enhance life to a better and more fulfilling stage. If things such as books, films or movies, preaching or messages, etc. can influence the thoughts of a person, then it can likewise influence an individual's lifestyle too.

What captivates or dominates the mind of a person can influence or control the person. People are not easily influenced from the outside, but from the inside by polluting the way they think or visualize things. A corrupted mindset gives birth to a corrupt person, so change the way a person thinks and you can change their entire lifestyle.

13 | CHANGE IS THE ONLY CONSTANT THING, AND IT BEGINS IN YOUR MIND

Change your thought process to change your lifestyle

Without a change in your mind it is impossible to experience change in your entire life. Change the way you think, and your life will definitely change. Change your thought process to change your lifestyle.

A change in your mindset from negative to positive will generate a change in your physical life. Someone who never takes any drastic steps to change from within the mind cannot make any change outwardly.

The change that happens in the mind is the only genuine change and can always reflect on the outside, for you cannot change except if you change your thought patterns.

Any change that is from the mind is permanent and transformative in nature. What you think is what you become in that instant. If a man cannot change his mindset, there is no force that can effect such change. A change in mindset can always help to break strong negative habits. Change is also the natural law of life.

 ENHANCING YOUR MIND WITH GOOD THOUGHTS IS WORTH MORE THAN ANY PHYSICAL ENHANCEMENT

The mind is key to everything that happens to us in life

Do not only spend money to adorn yourself with clothes, but enhance yourself with good thoughts. Good thoughts produce good and charming people in the world.

What you think reflects in your outfit. Thoughts aids decision-making that can make life beautiful, so control your thoughts to enjoy a good life. Positive and good thoughts can always move your life forward to attain great achievements and greatness which, in turn will, enhances your entire life with beauty and every good thing.

Whenever your mind is enhanced with positive thoughts it will translate to success and riches which, in turn, can enhance your physical life with material things such as clothes, cars, a house and any other good thing. If you enhance your mind with good thoughts, it will enhance your life with good things.

Bodily or physical enhancement fades away while good thoughts are life transforming because life is a byproduct of thoughts, or the physical manifestation of the mindset.

There is a need for every person to dominate their mind with good thoughts by adopting the right thinking patterns because you can never be what you never think in your mind. The human mind is a very functional component of our entire being. So, it is necessary to filter the inflow of your thoughts if success is your target in life.

Bear this truth in mind: that negative thoughts beget a negative life, while positive thoughts beget a positive life.

Likewise, virtues are the end result of a good mindset. All the individuals we see today on the planet reflect different mindsets, or ways of thinking. The mind is a department or component that controls our entire being, and any opportunity to succeed in life belongs only to those with enlightened mindsets really to make it to the top in life. The mind is the key to everything that happens to us in life. If things are good or bad, try to determine what dominates the mind.

The failure to refine your thoughts will directly affect your lifestyle because you can never be what you do not think. Maintain good thought faculties to be able to enter a healthy, positive and successful life. In a nutshell, what you think will always determine the direction of your life.

15 | SICK THOUGHTS PRODUCE SICK PEOPLE, WHILE HEALTHY THOUGHTS PRODUCE A STRONG GENERATION

Your thoughts can make you or break you

From my life experience, I discovered that you will remain sick if your mindset is tilted in the direction of sickness.

If you are thinking sick you will always appear sick. What you think in the mind is all that you appear in the physical.

For about twelve years of my life, I have been critically ill without any medical remedy, but the final solution came when there was a change from a 'sick' mentality to an all-round healthy mentality, which became the cure for the prolonged health challenge. You really become what runs through your mind, and then act the way you think and appear that way spontaneously.

A change of mentality can invariably change your health status. Sick thoughts produce sick people, while healthy thoughts will always produce healthy people. Healthy minds produce healthy bodies, and healthy people are products of healthy thoughts. But a sick mind automatically translates as a physically sick person. Mental and psychological ailments are what make people appear sick.

There is no sickness outside the mind that thinks sick thoughts. Always think healthy thoughts and there can be no force that can make you sick. If your thoughts are bedevilled, your life will be bedevilled. Health is of the mind and sickness is of the mind. Therefore, promoting healthy thoughts will help produce a healthy generation.

Your thoughts can make or break you. Sick thoughts produce sick people, and healthy thoughts produce healthy people.

The height of success is measured by the height of your thoughts

Nobody can accomplish their plans to their greatest extent, if your thoughts cannot see the goal.

The height you attain in life is measured by the height of your thoughts. Becoming great is the function of a great mind. How far you think is how far you can go in life.

Every great person thinks big and thinks about what they want to attain in life before reaching their goals. All goals, dreams, and aspirations are driven by a strong thought and desire to attain a particular position in life. How far you can see ahead determines how far you can go in life.

The ladder of success is not climbed physically, but by a strong projection in the mind. The higher you think, the higher you can climb the social ladder. The height of success is measured by the height of your thoughts.

The height of your thoughts determines the height you attain in life. Your thoughts are what carried you to where you are now, but can also keep you where you are. If you are able to project great heights, great things and success in your mind, it shows your ability for you to become successful. Any reality in the mind can be a reality in your life.

Seeing is the function of the mind not the eye

What you see with the mind is real and can stand the test of time. The mind can see wealth, riches and greatness in the invisible realm, while the natural eye can only see what is visible within your sight.

The mind is the faculty that controls our sight, while the eye is the organ that captures the image or picture only. The organ cannot function in isolation, away from the faculty that controls its functionality. The eye only sees the visible, while the mind sees the invisible. The eye sees only the object, while the mind sees its potential.

Those who see with their physical eyes get distracted by what they see, while those who see with the mind stay focussed on their vision, plans, goals and aspirations, and work towards fulfilling their destiny. Any time the mind is clouded with insignificant things, it will hamper the ability to project and visualize the future.

Always see with the mind to avoid limitation of your vision. If the mind is able to see something from the abstract world, it is possible to possess it in the physical world.

Don't be terrified by what the eye sees, but be encouraged by what the mind sees.

What you cannot see in your mind, you also cannot see physically. The mind determines what the eye is able to see. Seeing is the function of the mind, not the eyes.

Pure and well-guided thought to enable the fear of God

Without a mind that fears God, there is no fear of God. The fear of God is first established in the mind before physical obedience or demonstration.

The mind is where God resides, and submitting to His will begins in the mind. The mind predetermines the physical action.

Without a submissive thought, there will be no fear of God. God is not visible, so the fear of God is not a physical attribute, but strictly a function of the mind.

Pure and well-guided thought enables the fear of God. The only true way to fear God is through our thoughts.

 | CHANGING YOUR THOUGHT PATTERN IS ACCOMPANIED BY CHANGING POSITION AND LEVEL IN LIFE

An elevation of the mind is an elevation on the level of life

A positive change in mindset can also reposition your life. Changing levels requires a mature mindset, and a change to positive thoughts or mindset to promote your social status in life.

A mere salesman that changes the level of his thoughts can become the manager. The level of your achievement is proportionate to the level of your thoughts. An elevation of the mind is an elevation of your level in life.

Thinking big will make you grow in life to greater heights. A positive change in your thought pattern will affect a positive lifestyle which can stimulate growth and development. Whenever your thought pattern changes, your level in life will change in that direction, either positively or negatively.

Growth in mindset always accelerates growth in changing levels of life. Thoughts are transformative, so change in thoughts result in change in status.

Unhealthy thoughts can degenerate ill health

Any form of unforgiveness, bitterness, or grudge in the mind can break you down, which can result in ill health. Such thoughts attract stress and create a nervous condition in the body's chemistry, which can result in serious health issues.

The trauma or tension received by the body's system in response to such unhealthy thoughts can degenerate into ill health such as a stroke, ulcer, or paralysis, which are all negative effects of ill thoughts. In fact, your mental picture is your mental capability, and your mental capability is what gives strength to your body. If you feel bad at any time, just think well of yourself. An injury to your mind is an injury to your life.

What hurts your thoughts will hurt your future. A healthy life is determined by the state of your mind.

Once mindset is positive, possibility is always a reality

The mind that always thinks positively is capable of proffering solutions to every difficulty. People with positive mindsets never see anything as too difficult to achieve, and such mindsets always arrive at solutions to every difficulty. Examples are Thomas Edison and Michael Faraday. Once your mindset is positive, possibility is always a reality.

The positively minded person can also see a solution in every difficulty. This mindset believes that there is no problem without a solution. It understands that if there is no solution to any problem, such a problem will never exist.

This class of people believe that problems abound and that someone will be the solution provider, and that there is always a solution for every problem, which someone can convert into an achievement or success. A difficulty to you is not the same to another person because it could be very easy for someone else.

There is nothing called 'problem' or 'difficulty' in the realm of a positive mindset. Positive thinking conquers every obstacle and repositions your life above every barrier. The way you think determines how you can convert challenges into opportunities.

WHEN THE MINDSET IS NEGATIVE

A negative thought pattern is the enemy's greatest arrow,
it is shot at success and progress

A negative mindset reduces you to nothing and makes you operate in the realm of thought that nothing good comes your way. This kind of mindset makes a person become a nuisance in life.

A supposed great person will become irresponsible, and a liability to self and to others and in the long run, will accept mediocrity as the only alternative to survival. Due to negative thought, your entire destiny, goals and aspirations in your life will be submerged and can never be actualized at all.

Negative thought is dissimilar to success and fulfilment of destiny. It reflects a bad lifestyle, people often refer to their background or race as the problem. A negative thought pattern is the enemy's greatest arrow, it is shot at success and progress.

This thought pattern is the platform for every kind of failure in life. It can result in shattered dreams, and a lack of achieving the goals or targets meant to better the future. So, live positively to have a great future. Life is progressive in nature; don't think retrospectively because your future is determined by your thoughts.

The greatest enemy of a man is a negative thought pattern. Nobody is too bad to be transformed, except by a negative mindset. The greatest enemy of success is negative thought.

 | NEGATIVE THOUGHTS ARE THE FUEL OF DEPRESSION, FRUSTRATION, HYPERTENSION, ETC.

Frustration is also just a mindset, not a reality

A positive thought is the greatest counsellor, remedy and therapy. The greatest therapy for depression is positive thought, while negative thought is the fuel of depression.

Hypertension is also a product of negative thoughts, while positive thought is the therapy. Negative thoughts trigger or stimulate depression and hypertension, but positive thought is the cure.

The only way to avoid hypertension and depression is to begin to think positively. Frustration is also just a mindset, not a reality. A greater part of us lies in our thoughts rather than in the physical.

If you control your thoughts, you will have control over your actions

It is how you think that determines how you act, and actions are observable products of what we think.

Therefore, if you can control your thoughts, you will have control over your actions and life in general.

*Evil and good both originate from the mind and
translate as physical deeds*

This means you only manifest what you think, for the mind is the factory where good and bad are manufactured through thoughts.

The real you is embedded right inside your thoughts. So, evil and good both originate from the mind and translate into physical deeds.

It is right within the mind that both evil and good are first manufactured before their real exhibitions. The mind is the source of all evil, and the mind is the source of all good, so guide your mind.

Always think about possibilities

Limitation in the mind is already a limitation in life. There is nothing called 'limitation' in real life except the limit you create in your thoughts.

There are no walls or barriers to success other than the barriers created by your mind via your thoughts or imagination. Limitations or barriers are not a result of the physical, but of your thoughts or imagination through a negative mindset.

Except for when you create the barrier called limitation, you may never see one in your life. Always think about possibilities. Positive thinking conquers every obstacle and raises you above every barrier in life.

Removing barriers from the mind helps you to remove all barriers of limitations. You are where you are as a result of what you think.

Limitation in thoughts is a limitation in life. Stagnated thought leads to a stagnated destiny, and breakthrough thought leads to a breakthrough destiny. There is no such thing as failure, except the failure you have already established in your mind.

What always dominates your mind, will dominate your life. Great people never see limitations, but always see possibilities.

The oldest prison ever in the world is the prison of our thoughts

A negative mindset has caged, buried and imprisoned so many destinies which, ordinarily, are supposed to be great in life. As a result of negative thought, so many people die with their potential untapped. However, for those still alive, their potential is still lying dormant without any exploitation.

Due to negative thought patterns, many have gone to the grave with their raw potential and without making any meaningful impact in the world.

A negative mindset is the worst prison that ever existed in the history of mankind, which made so many supposedly great people live ordinary, mediocre lifestyles without defining a course of action for themselves.

The largest prison ever built in the world is the mind, which has imprisoned so many destinies. The oldest prison ever in the world is the prison of our thoughts. A negative thought pattern is the sworn enemy of success and greatness.

You manifest what you think

Negative thoughts may drag people into negative lifestyles such as drug abuse, alcoholism, prostitution and illicit sex, murder, robbery, and so on. Positive thoughts are more likely to produce positive qualities in a person such as a good personality, integrity, honesty, self-control and the fear of God.

The lifestyle of a person is defined by their mindset. Negative thoughts can produce a negative lifestyle, but positive thoughts can produce a positive lifestyle. Your lifestyle solidly depends on your type of thought pattern, or mindset, which culminates in a particular form of lifestyle, be it negative or positive.

Thoughts are like seeds, so sow good thoughts to reap good things in life; but if you sow bad thoughts, you shall reap bad things in life. There is no devil except the thoughts of a person where evil deeds are produced. A corrupt mind produces a corrupt ideology, but pure thoughts produce a pure ideology.

The mind of a person is a factory where good and bad are manufactured through thoughts. Evil is the product of a thought, but good is also the product of a thought. You manifest what you think. Think good thoughts to be good, and never think evil thoughts, or become evil.

 SHOW ME SOMEONE WHO ACCEPTS FAILURE, AND I WILL SHOW YOU SOMEONE OF NO RIGHT THOUGHT; BUT A GREAT THINKER IS ALWAYS SUCCESSFUL

Anytime a person fails, it is their mindset that has failed

A positive change in mindset can also reposition your life from failure to success. Quality thoughts will produce a successful personality. When, in your mind, you accept or think about failure in its physical form, you become a failure. This also directly applies as, 'show me someone who fails, and I will show you someone who does not think positively,' rather, than successful people who think positively.

Those who think negatively are automatically candidates for failure, but successful people always think positively.

Failure in the mind translates as failure in life.

Once the thought of discouragement kick-starts in the mind, the result in the physical realm is automatic failure. Sometimes it is a thought of fear of the unknown which later becomes failure.

Discouraging thoughts result in discouraging actions, and discouraging actions beget failure. The whole picture of what later becomes failure begins as a thought before actualizing itself in real life. Failure is always rather imagined than seen, but when it is established in the mind, it will manifest itself.

Setbacks are programmed in the mind by people, and it becomes a reality for them. Setback thoughts also become a meditation, and the meditation becomes failure, but removing setback thoughts from the mind is a sure victory over failure syndrome.

Anytime a person fails, it is their mindset that fails. Anyone who fails, first failed in their mind; and anyone who succeeds, first succeeded in their mind.

Failure is not an event or reality. Rather it is a form of negative imaginative forces that dominates the mindset and actualized itself in the life of the victim. Failure mindset or thought becomes failure while success mindset or thought becomes success in real terms. Thinking positive, means, living positive life. However, thinking negatively means living negatively, and living negatively means failure. Great and positive thinkers are successful, but those who don't think positively, or have a negative mindset, are mediocre or failures in life. Where did I fail in life? I will always ask my mind what happened!

No force can drag you backwards like dwelling on the past

Retrospective thought is the enemy of progress. The mindset of dwelling on the past is unprofitable and retrogressive to growth and productivity. No force can drag you backwards like dwelling on the past.

Thinking of the past will surely keep you in the past, and it reduces the strength of progress.

This lifestyle saps away the energy needed to invest in the future. The more you think about the past, the more it hinders you from projecting into the future.

So, the only force that keeps people in the past is retrospective thinking, mindset, or thought pattern. Unwise, unhealthy and corrupted thoughts are the greatest enemies of success.

The only force that keeps you in the past is the force of thought. If you continue to dwell on your past, your life will continue to be lived in the past. Life is progressive in nature, so stop thinking retrogressively.

THE POWER AND BENEFITS OF A POSITIVE MINDSET

31 | THE ONLY DIFFERENCE BETWEEN A LOCAL CHAMPION AND A SUPERSTAR IS THE MINDSET

Whatever you think, you become

The difference between a local champion and a superstar is the function of the mind. The latter's mindset is targeted at reaching higher and becoming a superstar, while the former's is to achieve at local level.

A superstar mindset makes a superstar, while the local champion mindset produces a local champion. The difference here is the ability to think and become the exact product of your thoughts. Whatever you think, you become.

Superstars are what they are because of the way they think, and the same applies to the local champion. Your thought patterns can attract promotion. At the same time, they can attract demotion. Thinking big is the lifestyle of superstars.

Thoughts are the secret behind ideas

It is thought that brought everything in to being. The entire universe and everything in it was first conceived in the mind of God via a thought before everything was created, or came in to being.

Nothing came to be without a deliberate and accurate thought in the mind of God the Creator.

Without thought, nothing can be created. Thoughts are the secrets behind ideas, and ideas are the secrets behind creation. What we think is what we create; and what we don't think, we do not create. Thought originates from God, and thought creates all things.

 | THE ENTIRE LIFE OF SOMEONE IS
THE SUM OF THEIR THOUGHTS

Never dream to become what you do not think

A change in your mindset can also reposition your life. Quality thoughts can produce quality people and personalities. The person is their thought, and thought is the person. It can be better said that your existence is the sum of your thoughts.

What we think and how we think is all that we become; there is no addition or subtraction. A thought plus a thought is equal to the person, but if you subtract a thought of someone from them, it will equal no one.

Everyone is the direct product of their thoughts. Show me someone, and I will show you how they think. Someone who thinks positively will reflect it in a positive lifestyle, but someone who thinks negatively will reflect it in a negative lifestyle. Never dream to become what you do not think in your mind.

People always reflect what they think in words and actions alike. Your mind is essential to your survival as a successful being. The mind is the person, and the mind is the entire being of the person.

The whole existence of mankind is summarized in thought or mindset. Your mind possesses your whole being; a foolish desire in the mind begets a foolish action.

 NATURAL FORCES ARE ATTRACTED TO YOU
BY YOUR THOUGHTS: BLESSINGS OR CURSES

Every natural force is attracted to a thought pattern

Thoughts can attract blessings or curses. Positive thoughts attract blessings, but negative thoughts attract curses. If you think about blessings, you will receive blessings; but if you think about curses, you will receive curses.

Your thought patterns will determine what results to get from your thoughts; either a bad or good reward. Every natural force is attracted to a thought pattern. Just decide what to think in order to enjoy a corresponding result, be it blessings or curses.

Everything good or bad is the product of a thought. Every action is the product of a thought, be it good or bad. Actions will attract blessings or curses.

What the mind attracts can also attract your attention, be it blessing or curses. To conclude, thoughts determine what natural forces you attract; either blessings or curses.

*With positive thought, every mountain is surmountable, and
every desert can turn in to arable land*

The mind turns a desert in to arable land and levels mountains. The mind converts the impossible to the possible, difficulties to opportunities, lack to abundance, hardship to entrepreneurship, disappointment to blessings, and closed doors to opportunities to exploit greatly.

Change your thought patterns from negative to positive, and every problem will become surmountable. A positive mindset can convert every deteriorating situation into a healthy one.

With positive thought, every mountain is surmountable, every desert can turn in to arable land, and every valley becomes flat land.

A practical illustration of a desert turning into arable land is the thriving agriculture of the nation of Israel, and other Middle Eastern nations. However, an abstract illustration is the desert land of Dubai, which is the greatest tourist centre of the world today.

A natural phenomenon does not matter. However, the mentality of the inhabitant of a place matters far more in the world of positivism.

Toyota's slogan was, "Good thinking. Good product," which means no good thing ever existed without the production of a good thought.

The mind is a factory where every product is manufactured before the physical product comes to exist

Quality thoughts produce quality products. Good things will always come as a result of positive thinking. The capacity to think positively can generate good things such as ideas, concepts, innovations and inventions.

In a brief illustration is Toyota's cars, which are more economical and easy to maintain by their users than many other cars. Good products are only possible in the realm of positive thinking or mindset. Those who think creatively can always create new things out of nothing.

Every product is first manufactured in the mind before the real-life product in the market.

A product established in the mind is a reality in the material world.

The mind is a factory where every product is first manufactured before the physical product exists. The first stage of every good product begins in the mind before the final product is produced.

HEIGHT IS MEASURED BY THOUGHTS, AND GREAT HEIGHT IS A QUALITY OF A GREAT MIND

Sight is not the function of the physical eye, but of the mind and how high it can see

In the world of positive living, and in the realm of the mind, your physical height does not determine the height of the success you can attain in life.

Physical height is not the measurement for the height of achievement. In the realm of the mind, someone short could be as tall as the palm tree; but vice versa, a tall person can be short in the realm of the mind.

In this world, height (success) is determined by the level of your thoughts. This means that height is a quality of a great mind, instead of a physically tall person who thinks 'small'. A mentally tall person is more successful than a physically tall person.

Height is not the function of the physical structure, but the height that the mind can see. The physically tall can be defeated by a physically short person, who is tall in their mind.

Stand tall among the crowd by distinguishing yourself.

The true giants in life are the strong at heart and in mind.

*Both man and woman are destined for greatness, depending
on their mentality or mindset*

Greatness is not a function of gender, but is determined by mindset. Men and women have the prospect to become successful, depending on their mindset and how formidable his or her thoughts are.

Gender is not the yardstick for measuring greatness. All forms of disparity are not enough reason for failure. Both men and women are both destined for greatness, depending on their mentality or mindset.

If a man or woman thinks in terms of greatness, he or she can become great. It is the way you think that discriminates against your becoming successful, and not gender disparity.

Positive thinking removes every barrier of differences, and raises you high on the path of success. No man or woman should see gender as the criteria for becoming a success or failure. Only your thought faculties are your greatest liberty for success or greatness.

*We don't need riches to build the richest city, but great people
with a rich mentality*

A great mind is an asset, while money is the available resource to facilitate activities. The mind conceives the idea, and the idea becomes the visible city walls in action. No idea means no city. No money can conceive the idea, only the mind.

Where great minds exist, great things happen. Every beautiful city is first conceived in the mind. Model cities are products of models envisioned in the mental world via great thought patterns. Great minds create great thought patterns.

Great minds physically create plans already established as a mental picture. We don't need riches to build the richest city, but we need great people with rich mentalities.

Every great or model city is a product of great minds. Remember that they are the same great minds that create wealth or riches. To become rich is to start thinking rich, so it applies to a city too.

A lying mind is more destructive than a lie told

A lie is told to deceive another person, but the mind is capable of deceiving you (That is, people lie to deceive others, but the mind deceives you).

It is possible to detect a lie told, but quite difficult to detect self-deception that comes from the mind. It is very easy to correct a lie, but it's not easy to change the deceptive nature of your mind. A lying mind is more destructive than a lie told.

The mind may lie to you, till your death, through wrong actions. There is no witness against the lie of the mind. The mind is the most deceptive organ of a human being.

Only our thoughts can deceive forever, but others can only do it temporarily.

All other forms of lying or deception are temporary except the form in the mind which can cause grievous impact on our lives.

A positive mindset leads to inventions and creation

The best car ever invented or manufactured is not the car itself, but the thought that invented the car. If there is no thought, there can be no car. So, to admire any exotic car ever seen on the road is invariably to admire the mindset that produced such a car.

It means that a positive mindset leads to inventions and creations. The greatest car in the history of invention is a product of a positive mindset.

If the mind is able to invent something in its own realm, it is possible to possess it in the physical world.

The best vehicle or car ever invented is a product of the mind. Henry Ford invented the first car through the imaginative power of his thoughts before the physical product came to be. All cars are products of mindset.

A country without great minds will never attain greatness

A great nation emerges where there are great minds; not necessarily a country with a high population. Think of the USA, European countries, China, etc. that are controlling the world today. It is the hard work of great people who have great minds. Examples are Bill Gates, Henry Ford, and Thomas Edison who are better than billions of people in the world's population with negative mindsets.

A country without great minds will never attain greatness. Greatness is not the function of the availability of resources, but purely a function of the availability of great minds who can convert these resources in to material things.

Many great nations of the world are built by positive mindsets, but are not subject to an abundance of resources in their countries. Every country needs great minds for a real transformation to take place.

Only positive-thinking people can make a great nation. Quality thoughts produce quality people, who can make a great nation. All a country needs for transformation are great minds.

How positively you think can measure how productive you are

A positive change in your mindset can also reposition your life. What your mind possesses becomes your future. What you think and how you think today can determine your future either positively or negatively.

The ability to think positively means that you have the capacity to plan well for the future. Thought can project into the future.

Without positive thinking, there will be no meaningful future. How positively you think can measure how productive you are.

Analytical thinking can analyse future events and the way they will unfold. No future is a mere accident, but is determined through proper planning in the mind. Quality thoughts produce quality futures.

You can never be productive until your mind is productive. You will only have a rewarding future if you have a productive mind.

A sound mindset can also produce a vibrant person

Ask yourself: Are we the direct products of our thoughts because actions are synonymous with thoughts? To every thought there is a corresponding action. Only what you think can propel and spur you in to an action that resembles what is embedded within the mindset.

An aggressive mindset or thought will make a person act aggressively, but a calm thought or mindset makes a person act gently and calmly. Before anybody starts to behave in a particular manner, there must be a thought in the mind to do so. An action is not permitted to take place in the absence of a thought that must precede it. A sound mindset can also produce a vibrant person; and how mature you think determines the maturity of your actions.

Wise and responsible thoughts will produce wise and responsible actions. Doing things in the right way will involve a lot of thinking in the right direction. You are as liable for your thoughts as you are liable for your action. So, control your thoughts and ask yourself what you think about frequently, and you will know the reason you behave the way you do. Things can never be done the right way until people start thinking right.

Thoughts give birth to actions. The way you think is the way you act. In other words, what you think in the mind triggers your physical actions. Thoughts are like guns in a sense that they ignite every action taken by a person.

For example, there is no quarrel until one is conceived in the mind before the real act. When the mind immediately shoots a thought, there is always a sharp external reaction or response. To every thought, there is a corresponding action, and only thoughts stimulate or spur you in to action.

NO FORCE CAN KEEP YOU DOWN THE MOMENT YOUR THOUGHTS ARE ELEVATED

How positively you think can measure how productive you are

Your thoughts stand high on the peak of every success you can attain or achieve in life. The ability to subdue your thoughts is the ability to subdue the forces or pressures of life. The level your thoughts can attain equals the level you can attain in life.

Success is measured in the ability to think higher and uprightly. Awkward thoughts result in distorted growth, while positive thoughts lift people to greater heights in life.

When your thoughts are high, nothing can bring you down. How elevated your thoughts are will determine how great your achievements are. Higher goals lead to higher success.

The things that can bring your thoughts so low can drag you down to mediocrity, and result in failures too. The lowest point in life is not a low qualification, but the low mentality you may possess. There is no resistant force like the force of thought.

The strongest force in the world is the force of thoughts. There is no force that can keep you down except the force of negative thought. The moment you are lifted by your thoughts, there is no force that can keep you down. Positive thinking conquers every obstacle and raises you above every barrier in life.

Actions are direct products of your thoughts

Actions are triggered by thoughts, but at the same time, can destroy them. Any action created by your thoughts can also be destroyed by the same thought. It determines the power to start and stop, or change any action predetermined by the thought.

What can corrupt and destroy you is the way you think.

Thoughts are creative. They can create a situation and destroy it. Thoughts have the ability to spur you on, but also to discourage you.

Reset your thoughts to reset every action you take. Actions are direct products of your thoughts.

What you think can influence your actions

If you think rich, you will become rich; and if you think poverty, you will become poor. What you think will determine your actions. What enters the mind as a thought, determines the outcome through various actions.

What you think will determine your actions towards actualizing your goals and objectives. Clean thoughts will keep you clean, healthy thoughts will keep you healthy, and moral thoughts will keep you morally sound.

Thoughts are programmes. What you see in the mind is what you receive as an action. Human thoughts are like computer programs where your input determines your output. What you think influences your actions.

Filtered thoughts yield to a great personality

Anybody who is capable of purifying and sifting the kind of thoughts that run through the mind will definitely reflect that in life generally.

A good thought can produce a good person and, likewise, a bad thought can produce a bad person. If your thoughts are properly filtered, they will, in turn, produce a refined person who is capable of making remarkable success in life.

Filtered thoughts may yield a great personality.

The ability to filter thoughts influences your thought patterns and, at the same time, somehow rejects certain thoughts.

It also restricts unwanted ideas from occupying your mindset. It is a deliberate effort to remove garbage, or polluted ideas, from the mind so that positive thoughts can dominate. Removing barriers from the mind may help to decongest the thought faculties from bad and unprofitable ideas, or a negative mindset. The first step of precaution against anything bad is to warn the mindset.

Establish things in your mind and they will be established in your life

Any perspective in which the mind is able to view the world, either in the negative or positive, will automatically become its perception about the world.

What your mind perceives is what you see and get from the world. If the mind perceives doom, your entire life will be doom. The same applies to the way in which your mind perceives sickness, hardship or poverty. You will begin to see the world like that, and all you receive will be directly proportional to your mindset.

If you think about hatred all the time, you will always be treated with hatred by people. The same applies if you always think about love.

The principle of reciprocity can apply in this kind of mindset, either to the positive or negative. Establish something in your mind and it will be established in your life.

Negative thoughts attract negative circumstances. What you perceive in the mind is what you should expect to get from the world.

Remodelling your thought patterns will reflect in your life

Reactivating your thoughts means repositioning your life. It also means reactivating your life for the better. A remodelling of the mind attracts a repositioning and change of level in life.

Remodelling your thought patterns will reflect in your life. Any form of rebranding, reinvigoration, renovation, reviving and restoration that takes place within the mental faculties will definitely apply to your entire life.

Remodelling has to do with adding quality to your mindset so as to add quality to your entire life. This new model will affect your business, career, education and the totality of your being. Refining your thoughts means refining your decisions.

Those who think great become great, and vice versa

If you change your thoughts from acceptance of being an ordinary person to being a great one, there will also be a corresponding change in status. Those who think great become great, and vice versa. A great mind always thinks about great things or achievements, while a narrow mind will always settle for the little things.

The difference between Bill Gates and an ordinary person lies in their mentalities. Bill Gates thinks big and positive thoughts, while an ordinary person thinks small and negative thoughts. There are always various levels of thought patterns which produce various levels of people and achievements.

The narrow minds achieve small things, according to the measure of their thoughts; while great minds achieve greater things, according to the measure of their thoughts.

Talents and gifts are not enough reason for the difference, but it all boils down to the kind of mindset an individual adopts, which can really differentiate an achiever from a failure, or from being mediocre. The achiever thinks it is possible, but the mediocre think it is impossible. The great person can see the big picture, while the ordinary person can have only a narrow view.

The difference in thought patterns is what makes all the difference on the social ladder. You cannot do or become what you don't know, and you can only do or become what you do know.

Poverty is first established in the mind before becoming poor in life.

Poverty is not a personality. It is also not something material that you can see, feel or touch. It is just a product of a negative mindset. The difference between a great person and an ordinary person is awareness.

If there is no vision, there will be no mission

The mental feature arrives before the physical structure. There is always a concept, idea, or vision before the mission. The mind will always think it before the senses act upon it.

The mind first conceptualizes and visualizes before a physical structure is erected. Permit me to say that the skyscraper is first born in your thoughts before the physical edifice is constructed.

If the structure makes you marvel, please first marvel at the mind that produced the invisible image of the tall and admirable structure before any site work commenced.

Every skyscraper emerges from the thoughts of great thinkers. Each skyscraper is built in the mind first, and not with bricks. Whatever the mind thinks can be a reality.

Life is strictly and wholly controlled in the realm of the invisible

Life is fully controlled in the realm of the invisible. Every victory in the visible world is first won in the invisible world.

The physical world is the product of the invisible world. If the mind is able to see something in the abstract world, it is possible to possess it in the physical world. The positive realm of the mind is essential for a successful lifestyle.

Abstract thoughts determine the strength of your faith. Abstract thinking is the power behind inspirations, innovation, inventions, and every great idea in the world. Spur your thoughts on in order to spur your life on. The power of positive thinking is derived from the realm of the invisible.

Life is strictly and wholly controlled in the realm of the invisible. The way you see the world depends on the way you perceive it from the invisible.

The ability to see from the invisible can sustain your focus towards achieving goals and aspirations. Think abstractly to draw strength from the invisible world.

*What is not established in your mind cannot be achieved in
your life*

Awareness cannot take place if the mind is absent. An enlightened mind results in an enlightened person.

The only medium of awareness is from the readiness of the mind. Once the medium accepts and starts the process, then you reflect it outwardly in your life. It is in the mind that the ability of enlightenment lies.

A sound desire in the mind translates as sound deeds. Nothing can shape your life more than your thoughts. The greatest teacher of all time is your thoughts. What is not established in your mind cannot be achieved in your life. If only you could change from within then the change from outside would be very easy.

Reactivating your thoughts means reactivating your life for the better. A winner in thought is a winner in life because you become aware. If you get things right in your mind, you will get things right in life.

Life is a reflection of the readiness that exists in your mind. The level of your awareness in life can make you immune to any uncertainty that may befall you in the future.

Success first originates in the mind and
then metamorphizes in to reality

What exists as possible in the mind is already possible in real life. It is because your thoughts give birth to every reality in life. So, anything that is not possible in the mind can never be possible in life. The origin of every possibility is from the realm of the mind through the thought process.

Thought activates the act of possibility in the mind for it to become a reality in life. Once a thing is possible within the mindset, it immediately manifests as a possible event in the individual's life. So, thought precedes possibility and possibility fertilizes success, while success becomes greatness.

The mind first imagines something and it becomes possible in our lives. What the mind possesses becomes your passion in life. In the deep pit of impossibility, the only rescue is positive thought. Even when I don't have anyone to take me to the top, my thoughts can take me to the highest height in life.

Success first originates in the mind and the metamorphoses in to reality. Every act or deed begins in the mind. You can never influence anyone until you are able to influence their mindset.

If your mindset is changed, the change towards possibility is easy. Possibility is a reality, but nothing is possible except when you change the way you think. The best way to succeed is to believe in yourself.

Resisting defeat in the mind is resisting defeat in real life

If your mind accepts or thinks about defeat in the physical, you become defeated. Any defeat that occurs in the mind will definitely manifest in the physical. If you accept no defeat in the mind, then not even the greatest giant can intimidate you.

Physical defeat is a mere display of what is established in your mindset. There is nothing called defeat except the defeat you believe and have already bowed down to in your subconscious; in other words, your mind.

What you are able to subdue in your mind is already subdued in your life. If you have discovered yourself, you can never see defeat as an obstacle to destiny.

Resisting defeat in the mind is resisting defeat in real life (the physical). Defeat is from the mind and is not a physical factor.

So don't blame anybody for what happens to you in life

Never blame anyone for your misfortunes, predicaments, ideals and failures. Rather address them within your mindset, and redirect your thoughts in a positive direction. Success, progress, and greatness are products of a positive mindset.

Failure, hardship, and a low self-esteem are products of a negative mindset. What you think is what you become, how you think is what you get, and where your thoughts are now is where you will stay in life. Your thoughts define the course for positive or negative growth.

Nobody can keep you down when your thoughts are positive, and vice versa. To succeed is determined by your mindset; to fail is also determined by your mindset.

So, don't blame anybody for what happens to you in life. Narrow minds look at what others can do for them, or what people do against them. But great minds look for what to do for others.

Just stop fighting or blaming others as the cause of your predicaments. Rather blame the way you think. Fine-tune your mindset and every success can be achievable.

Your thoughts can make you a celebrity or a spectator in life

Every victory must begin in a convincing thought within you and then translate as physical victory. If you never conceive one in your mind, it means you can never see one in the real life.

There is a need for you to believe, but firstly in your mind, for it to manifest in the physical.

Therefore, first celebrate in the mind in order to celebrate in life. Anyone who celebrates in their mind is the determinant for any spectacular happening around them.

Your thoughts can make you a celebrity, or a spectator in life. The victory you are able to secure in your mind can also be the same in the physical realm.

The issues of the future start in the mind before solutions abound

The way you activate your thoughts positively can shape your future because the mind is the master of your life. The kind of mindset you possess is the key to how you plan your life towards the future.

How effectively and efficiently the mind is put to use will surely have a positive impact on your future. Envision your plans in your mind. Align your plans properly in your mind based on the kind of future you expect, and it will immediately reflect on your future. A positive thought in the form of a plan can enhance the future greatly.

Your thought patterns have the power to preserve or mar your future. The issues of the future start in the mind before solutions abound. To take hold of your thoughts, is to take hold of your future. Procrastination is the enemy of the future, and procrastination is a product of negative thought.

The entire idea about the future of everybody lies in the mind, so it depends on how the mind is being put to use to secure it. Your thoughts can really determine what you will be in future.

Your thought is your image

The candid truth is that people resemble their thoughts in actions, speech, facial expressions and physical appearance. In a nutshell, your life is summarized in the mind or thought.

Someone angry in their mind appears angry on their face. An 'untidy' mindset will affect the way you dress. A healthy mindset is expressed in a healthy lifestyle. Your thoughts appear in the form of actions, be they polite or aggressive.

Your mind is the functional part of you. What you think is all that people see in you. Whatever you see in a person, is thought in action. How kind and good you are does not originate as a facial expression, but in the mind. Who you are in your mind is the same person you are outwardly (your actions).

Your inner-countenance is portrayed in your outward appearance. Experiencing grief in your mind is to reflect grief facially.

Your lifestyle is simply a reflection of the way you think too. Your thoughts are a reflection of your self-image.

 DISPUTES CAN NEVER BE SETTLED UNLESS
FIRST SETTLED IN THE MIND

The entire peace process must begin in your mind

No amount of physical effort is capable of resolving disputes until the entire dispute is resolved in the mind in the form of a conviction to forgive and forget.

A dispute is first settled in the mind before the physical action to let the offender go is accomplished. If the mind is ready to let a matter go, the physical action will immediately be performed. In terms of any dispute, try to convince and address the mind and the entire dispute will be over.

THE CAPTOR OF THOUGHT IS THE CAPTOR OF CIRCUMSTANCE

A captive of thought is a captive in real life

To take control of your thoughts means that you can take hold of difficult situations. Your life is strictly and wholly controlled by the mind. The power of thinking is the power of life. To set your mind free means to set yourself free from any form of captivity. A captive of thought is a captive in real life.

If your thoughts are bedevilled, your life will be bedevilled. If your thoughts are liberated, then your life is equally liberated.

In the deep pit or prison of life, the only rescue is positive thought. What really kept you on the floor for so long is your thought or mindset.

You are the direct product of your thoughts. What captures your thoughts is the captor of your life. If you capture the mind, you will capture the person. The mind determines the relevance of a person.

What you think in your mind prompts your actions in the physical

Whatever you propose in the mind is what you will execute. We do what we think in our minds. What the mind is set to do is a reality in life. The entire process of life is first predefined in the mind before it's a reality.

An intention in the mind is a reality in life. What is not an intention in the mind can never be a reality in your life. The mind's conviction is the basic principle that guides the realization of our goals. What did not occur in the mind cannot be possible in life. The entire course of life is primarily predetermined first in the mind. Anything the mind agrees upon is bound to succeed.

It means every happening in your life has its origin in your mind via a thought process. If you are mentally derailed, you will be physically derailed. Thoughts empower physical decisions in redefining the course of your life.

Thoughts are real. What you think is what you see. What you always think and see is all you become in life. A crime is first committed in the mind before the real action occurs.

What you think in your mind prompts your actions in the physical. Don't confuse your mind because it will equally confuse your life. The mind first purchases anything you want to buy before purchasing it in the market.

 | WITH THE MIND, A WISE MAN SEES;
WITH THE EYES, NATURAL MAN WALKS

To be blind in thought is to be blind in the direction of life

Wise people see with the mind, while ordinary people see with the eyes. The mind sees greatness, abilities and possibility; the physical eye sees the opposite. The mind sees only the depth of life, while the eyes see only the peripherals.

If you use the mind to see, there will be no distractions. The natural eye is distracted and affected by so many sights. What you see in the mind is what you receive physically. The eye sees the shadows, but the mind sees the substance.

The mind is the only true eye that can see with clear vision, irrespective of what your natural eyes cannot see. What you see in the mind is all you can expect to get and to actualize in life. If you are able to see increase in your mind, your life will definitely be holistic. To be blind in your thoughts is to be blind in the direction of life.

If you want to go far, never see with your mere eyes, but with the mind. You will first see my thoughts before you see me in action. The ability to see things is solely dependent on the mind and not the natural eyes. Stop seeing only those things around you and start to see beyond, so that your expectations can be achievable in life.

A sound mind is life to the body

Those who spend time thinking quality thoughts will always enjoy a good life in the future. Time spent on productive thinking will result in a productive lifestyle which will attract the good things of life in the future. Also strive to invest in positive thinking to harvest quality life in the future.

Quality thoughts produce a quality life. What affects the mind can also affect the entire being of a person. Any project embarked upon in improving the mindset will automatically affect life in general.

Any amount of time spent on quality thinking will translate to a quality and successful lifestyle. All viable projects or efforts taken to transforming the mind will also reflect in the physical life.

The greatest thing you need to succeed lies in your thoughts. Positive living is a result of positive thinking. Renovate your mind in order to renovate your life.

The mind is the power house, the centre of your being, your live wire and control tower, so guide your mind. Enriching your mind means enriching your entire life. A good mindset translates as a good personality. A sound mind is life to the body. Enhancing the mind means enhancing your life.

A positive result from the mind culminates in a positive result in life. If thoughts are properly planned, life will also be properly planned. Wise and successful people invest in positive thinking, which yields great wealth and success.

The centre of your thoughts is the centre of your life

Nothing gets the attention of a person except what is able to attract the mind. Whatever attracts the mind can ultimately attract attention. The entire ability to stay focussed, concentrated, or stable is in the mind. Whoever has an unstable mindset will have divided attention.

The ability to say no to something in the mind will also mean that such a thing can never gain attention from you. The strongest forces that struggle for our attention, such as love, sex and hatred, can never be unless they find a place in the mind first before attracting attention.

Focus, concentration and stability are purely the function of the mind. With the mind, you desire and like something. With the same mind, you become attracted to it.

The mind is the functional part of a person. What you think is all that you will find yourself doing. It is what you think that makes you behave the way you do.

The mind's desires always translate as action in an individual. Make sure your mind is properly guided against what can attract it because it will also define your attention.

Be stable in the mind so as to be stable in life. Your mind tells you where to go and where not to go because you will always go in the direction of your mind. Distances are covered by the mind and not by the physical body.

The physical will see a mere picture of a cigarette, a bottle of alcohol, or a man or woman, but the mind will interpret it through a desire for one to smoke, drink or have sex.

What the mind desires always translates as an action by the individual. The centre of your thought is the centre of your life. What attracts your mind will definitely attract you. A foolish desire in the mind produces a foolish action through concentration on the desire in the mind. Be stable in the mind so as to be stable in life.

Both wealth and poverty are mentalities

The only conducive atmosphere you need to succeed in life is an appropriate mindset. Thoughts are future assets if properly structured.

You are first rich in the mind before becoming rich in life. The progress of a person is purely a function of the mind.

To have the treasures of good thoughts means to have the treasures of a good life. The progress of a man is purely a function of the mind.

To have the treasures of good thoughts means to have the treasures of life's fortunes and wealth. Wealth is a mentality. Poverty is also a mentality.

Rich minds are rich people in society. If you think rich, you will become rich. If you think poor, you will become poor. Every business and every profitable venture is first conceived and planned in the mind before physical execution.

An excellent mindset will produce an excellent person

Excellence, success and positive thoughts are inseparable, like the New York 'Twin Towers'. Your ability for greatness has lain dormant inside you since birth, waiting for the day you will discover it, and the whole world will celebrate you.

It means that an excellent mindset will produce an excellent person. The quality of your thoughts will determine your level of excellence. Thoughts that are directed towards hard work will definitely reproduce themselves as excellent ventures.

It means that unless your thoughts are geared towards hard work and success, you can never experience excellence. How mature you think determines how mature you will act.

The height of your thoughts determines your level of achievements or class in society. Greatness begins in the mind and translates as a great person. Only the great at heart enjoy the most of this life.

Faith is a direct product of positive thought

A positive mindset is the fuel of faith. With a positive mindset, faith is produced and sustained. A prayer that is supported by a positive thought can produce faith and great results. The strength of your thoughts determines the strength of your faith.

There is no faith without the power of positive thinking. This book is intended to spur your faith on by activating a positive mindset. The eye of faith sees every mountain as surmountable. A relaxed mind, full of positive thoughts, is an encouraging atmosphere for faith to thrive.

Faith is first produced in the mind before there is any physical display of it. Faith is a direct product of positive thoughts.

Liberation is purely a mental function

If your thoughts are liberated, you will be totally liberated. The process of true liberation must start in the mind before action can occur.

Liberation is purely a mental function, which results in the awareness of a particular right that is infringed, deprived or suppressed. Lack of awareness about a right or opportunity is a great barrier. What you don't know and cannot see in the mind is impossible to enjoy.

Freedom is only real through a greater level of mental awareness. The awareness that began in the mind of Nelson Mandela brought about the total liberation of the Blacks in South Africa from the cruel hands of the apartheid government.

Mental slavery is worse than any form of slavery in the world. Ensure your mental liberty in order to enjoy social and political freedom.

If you can control your thoughts, you will have control over your life. The ability to subdue your thoughts is the ability to subdue the forces or pressures of life.

If you are liberated in your thoughts, then your freedom is already secured. Removing every barrier in the mind means removing every barrier of life.

Reactivating your thoughts means repositioning your life

A rebranded thought ultimately produces a changed person. Transforming the thought pattern produces a transformed person as an end result. I found that the secret to self-discovery it is in changing the way you think.

Refining thought patterns aids self-discovery. Nothing and no one can change you but your thoughts alone. The only self-discovery lies in a change in the way you think. So many people cease to live long before they physically die because they are dead in the mind. Success is a product of self-discovery, and self-discovery is the product of thought.

If self-discovery is to become a reality, the greatest counsel is to consult your thought faculties. Reactivating your thoughts means repositioning your life.

Your self-image depends on the way it is perceived in the mind. Great thoughts produce great people. Failure is the product of a thought, and success is the product of a thought. If you are seriously troubled, the greatest counsel is to consult your thought faculties.

Most successful people are optimistic thinkers

An optimistic mindset translates as material assets. Optimists are persistent in pursuing their goals. An optimist reaps where others have given up. Optimism is a firm conviction in the mind of a person.

Optimistic thoughts persist until a positive result is received from difficult situations. Most successful people are optimistic thinkers who see greatness and wealth where others quit. An optimistic mindset always operates in the realm of possibilities.

Their persistence can be converted into success and riches.

In situations where others quit, it becomes an opportunity for an optimist to exploit greatly and to make wealth. This kind of mentality is capable of displaying firmness in a discouraging situation by converting it into an opportunity.

The great cities of Dubai, Saudi Arabia and Israel are all located in the desert region of the Middle East, but they flourish in agriculture and wealth because of the great minds that exist there.

An optimistic mentality can convert a difficult and impossible situation into an opportunity for greatness.

Thoughts begin communication

Our human lives are better imagined in the thoughts of our minds. As thoughts add meaning to life, it makes the idea of communication possible. It can be simply put that, if there is no thought, there will be no communication.

This is because it is thought that generates the idea of communicating with one another. More clearly, thoughts begin communication, which means that communication originates as thoughts in the mind, and then become a process that can take place in actual life.

Think of any kind of communication that ever existed. It all began as a thought, without which life would become meaningless.

Our thoughts always start the communication process and, at the same time, can cause a break in the process if distorted in the mind. The mind initiates the communication process and the mind sustains it. You are indeed alive because your mind is alive.

The more the thought of love dominates the mind, the more love waxes stronger

Love is not a physical object and it does not originate from the physical. Love originates in the mind as a product of thought. If there is no thought of love that comes in the form of feelings from the mind, there will be no such thing as love. This means that every love process must emanate from the mind through a feeling of romance, and become an act of love between two or more attracted individuals.

The more the thought of love dominates the mind, the more love waxes stronger. This is the reason why love prevails even when the other party is physically absent. Tentatively, love is a magnetic force, residing within the mind of a person. Any love outside the mind is fictitious and not truly genuine.

True love henceforth comes from the mind before a display of physical romance. It is how you think that determines how you act in terms of love or romance with a person. Thoughts can attract or repel the company of a person.

You first become my friend in the mind before I approach you for friendship. The greatest energy or strength that sustains love or romance is just the thought about it.

*The higher you think, the higher you will go on the ladder
of success*

Where you are today is a result of a possessive mindset which brought you there. The ability to possess a position or level in your mind gives impetus to your determination to get there.

Whenever there is a thought in the mind, there is always the possibility of getting there. Every height you think about in the mind can be reachable, and a destination you thought of is as good as arriving there.

No one achieves what they did not conceive in the mind. Every business ambition or dream, and achievement must start in the mind as a thought for it to become a reality.

This means that the magnitude of your thoughts determines your position or level of greatness to attain in life.

The higher you think, the higher you will go on the ladder of success. The only secret to greatness or success lies is in the ability to empower your thought faculties. How far you think, determines the level of success you can attain in life.

A poor mentality determines where you are, while a rich mentality determines that you have not yet started. What the mind can possess becomes your possession.

If you direct your thoughts towards greatness, there will be a corresponding change in status. You can never get to the top if the mind never takes you to the top.

A defeatist in the mind is prey to the negative circumstance of life

Your mental picture is your mental capability, and your mental capability is your physical strength. A race is already won in the mind before the actual contest on the track takes place. Winners in the mind are winners in life. To fight negative thoughts from your mind is as good as successfully fighting all your life's battles triumphantly.

Fear and doubt are negative products of the mind or thought. Removing every barrier in your mind means removing every obstacle from your life.

The battle is first seen in our thoughts before the physical engagement in action or deeds occurs. Your mind possesses your every victory in the battle of life.

There are no lost battles except those the mind has imagined.

If you shoot your thoughts on top, you will always be on top of every situation in life. There is no resistant force like the force of thought.

The strength of your thoughts can determine the way you fight all of life's battles. The strongest person is not the one with physical might, but the one with a great mindset. What the mind has conquered can be conquered in real life.

What you believe is what will conquer you, and not what you see with your physical eyes. A battle is first won in the mind before the real battle at the battlefront occurs. A defeatist in the mind is prey to the negative circumstance of life.

Greatness has lain dormant inside you since birth, awaiting the way in which you will discover it for the world to celebrate you.

The mind is central to every affair of life, of every individual,
in its totality

The way you think is the way you act. The mind is the chief administrator and manager of your life. The mind manages the affairs of your life as it guides and directs the way you act or behave. The mind is the very key to decision-making with regards to the issues of life.

The mind as the live wire of your being, the centre of life's functionality and the brain box of everyone, can automatically coordinate the affairs of life. The simple reason is that the mind is key to every success or great thing. It also means that the mind is central to every affair of life, of every individual, in its totality.

This can simply be put this way: that the mind is the coordinator of your life affairs. The mind is also the manager of other resources, residing in the human system, such as the five sensory organs; the eyes, nose, skin, ears and tongue.

There is only one good manager that coordinates the affairs of your entire life and that is the mind. Learn not to live from the outside, but from the inside because the inside coordinates your activities in thought, speech, and action.

Conclusion

Thought is the oldest philosophy of life because every created thing emerged from a thought. The strength of thought is real, tested and proved. It possesses the power that is capable to direct the entire human body regarding in which direction to go.

The mind or human thought is directly connected to the realm of the spirit. All the control forces of human life operate within the territory of the mind. That makes it the master of life in general. The strongest person can be pulled down by the force of a single thought. People with a strong mindset are strong people. Every genuine change must be from the inside because what is inside must always reflect on the outside.

The thought faculties of humans are amongst the most crucial resources needed to be harnessed for the purpose of societal development and progress in the global arena. The thought patterns of so many individuals have deprived them the opportunity to maximize their potential and to attain greatness.

Pro-active quotes

1. The strongest force of violence in the world is a negative mindset.
2. The person inside you is the greatest enemy or friend to your success.
3. Where your mind is, there your treasure lies.
4. The depth of your understanding is located in the depth of your thoughts.
5. Every reality of life is found in your imagination. What you can imagine can become real in life.
6. Great thoughts produce greater achievements.
7. Incline your heart to your priorities and the result will be positive.
8. The greatest witchcraft is a negative mindset.
9. The forces that control the mind can control the utterances and actions of every person.

About the author

Raymond Delmut Na'anlep was born in 1976 to parents who are both peasant farmers with no form of formal education. He hails from Bwall Village in Qua'an pan Local Government Area in the plateau state.

He is the second child of a family of fifteen, including ten males and five females. All are still alive. He attended LEA Primary School in Goepil from 1985 to 1990, where he was the head boy of set 1990. He then attended Boys Secondary School (BSS) in Gindiri in plateau state from 1991 to 1997. He held the position of Labour Prefect.

He then went to the Federal Polytechnic in Nasarawa to study a diploma in public administration from 2004 to 2006. He also obtained a certificate in supervisory general management (CSGM) (2004/2005) from the Federal Training Centre (FTCK) in Kaduna before going back to complete his diploma at the Federal Polytechnic in Nasarawa in 2006.

Thereafter, he went back to the Federal Training Centre in Kaduna (FTCK) to complete another diploma in public administration from 2009-2011, where he jointly held the position of the honourable speaker of the student representative assembly (SRA). In 2014, he also obtained a higher diploma in public administration from the same institution. He then became the president of the students' union government (SUG), 2013-2014.

Delmut Na'anlep is a registered member of the Abuja Writers Forum (AWF), and a trained information technology professional. He is also a Microsoft certified Information Technology Professional (MCITP), and a Microsoft Certified Solution Expert (MCSE).

He is presently working with the Ministry of Foreign Affairs in Abuja. The Author, of "THE MINDSET" is an Administrative Attaché, to the Nigeria High Commission in Pretoria, South Africa.

His hobbies include reading, writing, writing poems and poetry recitation, playing and watching football, and embarking on several adventures. He is happily married to a beautiful wife, Martina Raymond Na'anlep.

Reviewed note

The Mindset Authored by Raymond Delmut Na'anlep is such an important and fascinating book for everyone's daily consumption. The interpretation of how the human mind functions was adequately exonerated with a brilliant penetration of analysis. Certainly, the author carefully provoked those symptoms that found the ground base of human negativity in general. Perhaps, the choice of quotes in this book was practically kicked with an enduring clarity that will prove valuable to all readers of this book. Therefore, the piece of work contained in this book explained the heartbeat of the author's ultimate passion for human freedom internally once Men and Women could acknowledge the challenges they face daily. In this book, one will also figure out an obvious work of originality by "Raymond" and shaped by his experiences and determinations to lift off the burden of Mindset within the human mind. For those with doubts Mindset, this book brings you a stability of purpose toward an encouraging future. A pretty interpretation of Mindset vocabulary!

Dr Shaibu D. Sunday, PhD

Books, articles read & references

R. Luria (1968) The Mind of a Mnemonist; A Little Book about a Vast Memory.

Raymond E. Fancher (Author), Alexandra Rutherford, Pioneers of Psychology: A History (Fourth Edition) 4th Edition

Richards J. Heuer, Jr. (1999) Psychology of Intelligence Analysis

Carol S. Dweck, Ellen L. Leggett (1988) A Social-Cognitive Approach to Motivation and Personality.

Sigmund Freud (1916-1917) A general Introduction to psychoanalysis 130.

Confucius: The Doctrine of the mean, Violet M. Firth (1922) "Dion fortune" Kravitz, D. A., & Martin, B. (1986). Ringelmann rediscovered: The original article. Journal of Personality and Social Psychology, 50, 936–941.

Baron, R. (1986). Distraction/conflict theory: Progress and problems. In L. Berkowitz (Ed.), Advances in experimental social psychology (Vol. 19). New York, NY: Academic Press.

Triplett, N. (1898). The dynamogenic factors in pacemaking and competition.American Journal of Psychology, 9(4), 507– 533.

Stasser, G., Kerr, N. L., & Bray, R. M. (1982). The social psychology of jury deliberations: Structure, process, and product. In N. L. Kerr & R. M. Bray (Eds.), The psychology of the courtroom (pp. 221–256). New York, NY: Academic Press.

Baron, R. S. (2005). So right it's wrong: Groupthink and the ubiquitous nature of polarized group decision making. In M. P. Zanna (Ed.), Advances in experimental social psychology (Vol. 37, pp. 219–253). San Diego, CA: Elsevier Academic Press; Janis, I.

Nijstad, B. A., Stroebe, W., & Lodewijkx, H. F. M. (2006). The illusion of group productivity: A reduction of failures explanation. European Journal of Social Psychology, 36(1), 31–48; Stroebe, W.,

Diehl, M., & Abakoumkin, G. (1992). The illusion of group effectivity. Personality & Social Psychology Bulletin, 18(5), 643– 65.

L. (2007). Groupthink. In R. P. Vecchio (Ed.), Leadership: Understanding the dynamics of power and influence in organizations (2nd ed., pp. 157–169). Notre Dame, IN: University of Notre Dame Press.

THE MINDSET
A NOVEL

The mindset is a well-informed and inspiring book. The unique interpretation of how the mind functions is one modern magic that Raymond has brought on to intellectual stage. This book applies a coherent, challenging and sustained narrative of the whole picture of how the human mind functions. The primary purpose of this outstanding book is to give the reader an extraordinary new lease of life. In this book one will find a convincing analysis of how the human mind functions through modern day revelations regarding the influence of the human mind over the everyday life of all humans. Perhaps it has been proven that one cannot live everyday of one's life resembling another person like oneself. These insightful thoughts were not generated by an accident of time. They came about naturally. Indeed, this book authored by Raymond ought to change the mindset of everyone who reads it and it will support each individual in grasping the pictures of their daily life. For instance, how do you carry out a sustainable life and get maximum advantage out of situation and decisions that each human being make during their lifetime. It is obviously an astonishing and spectacular work of the prevailing time. Even so, this book is a brain back-up that every living person must check out for themselves and thus absorb its judicious and with unique counsel.

Other books by the author

Raymond's book *The Success Codes: The last Human Hope!* is an extraordinary and unique masterpiece which was envisioned to unravel, transform and to provide every individual the self-seeded support, and to inspire all the readers of this book with the power which is found within each human being while further strengthening their inner outlook to embrace openness to the modern societies without fear. In a very rare concept, this book is a versatile dictionary of knowledge at all times to be found in modern times. If you would like more information on Raymond's second book, or if you would like to order your copy, please contact the author via phone or email:

Phone number: 083 594 3281

Email: galaxymindsmediahouse@gmail.com

Website: www.galaxymindsmedia.com